1. Pacing Stallion.
2. Orloff Stallion.
3. Thoroughbred Stallion.
4. Pereberon Stallion.
5. Shire Stallion.

6. French Coach-Stallion.
7. Shetland Pony.
8. Hackney Stallion.
9. Cleveland Bay stallion.
10. Belgian Stallion.

11. Trotting Stallion.
12. Arab Stallion.
13. German Coach-Stallion.
14. Clydesdale Stallion.
15. Suffolk Stallion.

BUSHEL
& PECK
BOOKS

Text copyright © 2020 by Mifflin Lowe
Illustrations copyright © 2020 by Wiliam Luong

Published by Bushel & Peck Books, www.bushelandpeckbooks.com.

**Special thanks to our Book Angels, Karen M.
and Andew C., and to our newest friends:**

- *Black Reins Magazine:* An outstanding publication run by
  Stanford E. Moore celebrating the black cowboy community.
- **Rory Doyle Photography:** You have to see Rory's
  photographs. They're incredible.
- **The South Dakota Cowgirl:** A talented Western
  photographer. Go see her work!
- **Cheyenne Glade Wilson—***The Native Cowgirl*: An
  outstanding blog by Montana cowgirl Cheyenne Glad Wilson.

Bushel & Peck Books is dedicated to fighting illiteracy all over the world. For every
book we sell, we donate one to a child in need—book for book. To nominate a school or
organization to receive free books, please visit www.bushelandpeckbooks.com.

LCCN: 2019956092
ISBN: 9781733633512

First Edition

Printed in China

10 9 8 7 6 5 4 3

THE TRUE WEST

REAL STORIES ABOUT
BLACK COWBOYS, WOMEN SHARPSHOOTERS,
NATIVE AMERICAN RODEO STARS, PIONEERING
VAQUEROS, AND THE UNSUNG EXPLORERS,
BUILDERS, AND HEROES WHO SHAPED
THE AMERICAN WEST

BY **MIFFLIN LOWE**

ILLUSTRATIONS BY **WILIAM LUONG**

CONTENTS

COWHAND   LAWMAN

EXPLORER   LEADER

ENTERTAINER   BUILDER

SOLDIER   SOCIAL TRAILBLAZER

AUTHOR'S NOTE
THE WESTERN MELTING POT

This is the page that nobody ever reads, but this time, I hope they will! I've written this book in hopes that its stories—and the incredible people they're about—will pull our country closer together through a shared history of the American West. In its own way, the Wild West was a melting pot every bit as much as the cities of the East Coast—and maybe even more so.

While the American cowboy is, deservedly, a cultural icon and part of our national mythology, what many people don't know is that a significant percentage of America's cowboys were African American, Latino, and Native American. Many cowboys were even . . . cowgirls. I hope that Americans from every part of our country come to understand and appreciate the fact that the people who settled the West weren't all just "Marlboro men." They were, in truth, everybody—people from every race, gender, and ethnicity who built, explored, and fought to make the West what it is today. In one way or another, every one of them was a pioneer, and they are all part of our heritage.

As we examine the lives of each of these individuals, we must recognize that many of them achieved all this in the face of social opposition and prejudice. Native American tribes suffered enormously from the westward expansion of the United States. Black cowboys were often given the dirtiest jobs. Chinese railroad workers faced unbelievable conditions and national scorn. Yet in spite of it all, these brave men and women helped create the country that we live in today. This is truly a story that can unite us all.

I think the parents, teachers, librarians, and, most of all, the kids who read this book will enjoy the amazing stories of the people on the American frontier. These people were strong, smart, tough, and astonishingly resilient. Above all, I hope that everyone who reads this book (and looks at the great pictures) will carry a knowledge of the history this book reveals in their hearts throughout their lives, and with it, an appreciation for their fellow Americans from every background.

—MIFFLIN LOWE

AND GOOD GUIDELINES FOR EVERYONE, DON'T YOU THINK?

COWBOY & COWGIRL CODE

ALWAYS TELL THE TRUTH.

FINISH WHAT YOU START.

WHEN YOU MAKE A PROMISE, KEEP IT.

TAKE PRIDE IN YOUR WORK.

BE GENTLE WITH CHILDREN,
ANIMALS, AND OLDER PEOPLE.

RESPECT OTHERS IF YOU WANT
TO BE RESPECTED.

DON'T BE LAZY.

DON'T BRAG OR SHOW OFF.

BE NEAT, CLEAN, AND TAKE
CARE OF YOUR BODY.

TALK LESS AND SAY MORE.

NICK NAME: THE DUSKY DEMON

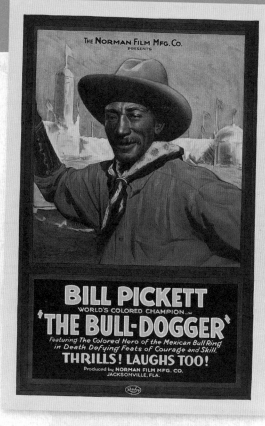

Imagine riding a horse* while chasing a longhorn steer with six-foot horns across a rodeo ring. Now imagine jumping off your horse, grabbing the steer by its horns, twisting its head up to the sky and then . . . biting the longhorn on its upper lip as you wrestle it to the ground!** That's what the famous rodeo cowboy, Bill Pickett, did as a star in the 101 Ranch Wild West Show, an incredible show that included other legends like Buffalo Bill, Will Rogers, and Tom Mix. It took immense nerve and strength to wrestle with a bull that could weigh as much as a ton, but astonishingly, Bill was only five-foot-seven and weighed about 145 pounds.

Bulldogging wasn't the only amazing accomplishment of Bill's life. Born in 1870, he began his cowboy career while he was still in fifth grade. Showing off his roping and riding, Bill passed a hat for donations, and people were glad to give. As he grew up, Bill and his four brothers performed tricks and stunts at country fairs all across the West. He eventually joined the 101 Ranch show and performed there and other places for over twenty-five years.

As well as an incredible cowboy, Bill Pickett was one of the first black movie stars, known as "The Dusky Demon."

IN HIS OWN WORDS:

"WHAT'S GONNA HAPPEN, GONNA HAPPEN . . ."

(WHAT BILL SAID TO HIMSELF BEFORE GOING FACE-TO-FACE WITH A BULL.)

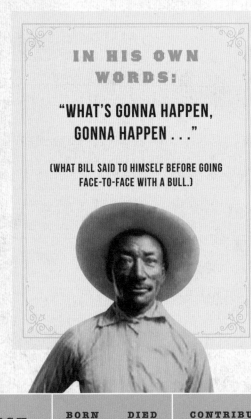

Despite bulldogging year after year, Bill somehow managed to keep his teeth and still have such a great smile that he became one of the first black movie stars. He appeared in the films *The Bull-Dogger* and *The Crimson Skull*.

Sadly, Bill died after he retired when he was kicked in the head, not by a steer, but by a horse. On his radio show, famed humorist Will Rogers, who had been Pickett's partner in the rodeo, announced the passing of his good friend to the entire nation.

Mr. Pickett was inducted into the Rodeo Hall of Fame of the National Cowboy and Western Heritage Museum in 1971. In 1989, he was inducted into the Pro Rodeo Hall of Fame, and in 1993, the United States Postal Service included Bill Pickett in the "Legends of the West" commemorative sheet of stamps. Finally, in 2017, his hometown of Taylor, Texas, erected a statue of Bill Pickett and named the street that leads to the rodeo arena in his honor—an honor remarkably earned.

*PICKETT'S HORSE WAS NAMED SPRADLEY.

**HE GOT THE IDEA FROM BULLDOGS THAT USED TO DO THIS ON CATTLE DRIVES.

QUICK FACTS

BORN	DIED	CONTRIBUTIONS
1870	1932	INVENTOR OF BULLDOGGING, MOVIE STAR.

STATE: OKLAHOMA

OKLAHOMA, WHERE BILL PICKETT DIED, IS HOME TO THE NATIONAL COWBOY AND WESTERN HERITAGE MUSEUM.

DID YOU KNOW?

Bill Pickett's films were all silent films. During his time, audiences would watch the movies while a pianist or organist played music in the background at the theater.

Bulls used in bulldogging usually weighed between 650 and 700 pounds. Can you imagine bringing *that* down with your bare hands?

Annie Oakley was a huge star.* But she sure didn't start out that way.

Annie grew up poor, working as a servant and trapping animals to help feed her family. Her life changed, however, when eight-year-old Annie shot a rifle and hit her target—dead center. As a teenager, she hunted and sold meat to pay her mom's mortgage. Then, at age fifteen, Annie won a match against a professional sharpshooter, took home the $100 prize, and was on the road to her amazing career.

In Buffalo Bill's Wild West show, Annie was paid more than any other performer. She shot over her shoulder by looking in a mirror, shot from the back of a galloping horse, and even hit dimes thrown in the air!

Annie became America's first woman celebrity.

BUFFALO BILL'S WILD WEST.
CONGRESS, ROUGH RIDERS OF THE WORLD.

MISS ANNIE OAKLEY,
THE PEERLESS LADY WING-SHOT.

Performing for enormous crowds and European royalty, Annie became America's first woman celebrity. England's Queen Victoria, Italy's King Umberto, and Germany's Kaiser Wilhelm II were all fans, and the king of Senegal even invited Annie to come control his country's tiger population.

Annie strongly supported women's rights and pressed for women to be independent and educated. She firmly believing that a women could do anything a man could. Annie also thought it was important for women to learn how to use guns to defend themselves. She taught more than 15,000 women to shoot, saying, "I would like to see every woman know how to handle guns as naturally as they know how to handle babies."

To serve her country, Annie also offered to provide fifty female sharpshooters to fight in the Spanish-American War, volunteered to train women to fight in World War I, and visited Army camps to raise money for the Red Cross.

In 1894, Annie performed in one of Thomas Edison's first films: *The Little Sure Shot of the Wild West.*** Ever since, she's been the subject of plays, movies, television shows, and the Broadway smash, *Annie Get Your Gun.*

A member of the Trapshooting Hall of Fame, the National Cowgirl Museum and Hall of Fame, and the National Women's Hall of Fame, Annie's legend lives on today—and will live on forever.

*ACTUALLY, SHE WAS A LITTLE STAR—SHE NEVER GOT OVER FIVE FEET TALL!

**ANNIE WAS GIVEN THE NICKNAME OF *WATANYA CICILLA*—"LITTLE SURE SHOT"—BY FELLOW PERFORMER SITTING BULL.

QUICK FACTS	BORN 1860	DIED 1926	CONTRIBUTIONS	STATE: OHIO
			SHARPSHOOTER, PERFORMER, FIGHTER FOR WOMEN'S RIGHTS, AMERICA'S FIRST WOMAN CELEBRITY.	OHIO, WHERE ANNIE WAS BORN, IS THE ONLY STATE WITH A PENNANT-SHAPED FLAG. IT WAS ALSO THE FIRST STATE TO PROTECT WORKING WOMEN.

IN HER OWN WORDS:

"AIM AT THE HIGH MARK AND YOU WILL HIT IT. NO, NOT THE FIRST TIME, NOT THE SECOND TIME, AND MAYBE NOT THE THIRD. BUT KEEP SHOOTING— AND FINALLY YOU'LL HIT THE BULL'S-EYE OF SUCCESS."

DID YOU KNOW?

Thomas Edison—known for inventing the light bulb and the phonograph—also created one of the first video cameras. To keep his invention popular, his company produced a variety of films, one of which starred Annie Oakley.

Annie could split a playing card—held sideways—from thirty paces away!

NICK NAME: DEADWOOD DICK

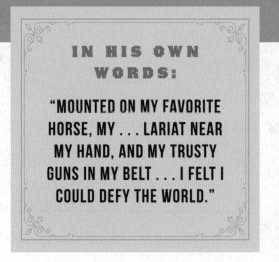

IN HIS OWN WORDS:

"MOUNTED ON MY FAVORITE HORSE, MY . . . LARIAT NEAR MY HAND, AND MY TRUSTY GUNS IN MY BELT . . . I FELT I COULD DEFY THE WORLD."

As well having one of the coolest nicknames in the Wild West, Nat Love, known as "Deadwood Dick," was also one of the coolest looking dudes on the frontier. He let his hair grow long, topped it off with a hat sporting a pushed-up brim, and wore a stylish neckerchief around his neck.

Born in 1854 in Tennessee, Nat was taught to read and write by his father, a foreman on a plantation, even though laws before the Civil War didn't allow blacks to do this. Later, as a teenager, Nat demonstrated a talent for training wild horses. Then, at age sixteen, after winning $50 in a lottery, Nat headed West. He worked on the 125,000-acre Duval Ranch in Texas, where he learned how to rope, brand, and herd cattle. He also became an expert with firearms and fought cattle rustlers.* Once, while rounding up stray cattle, he was shot several times and captured by a band of Pima Indians. Afterwards, the Pima nursed him back to health and wanted to adopt him into the tribe. Instead, Nat stole a pony and escaped.

Nat wrote about his experiences in his very own autobiography called *The Life and Adventures of Nat Love.*

In 1872, Nat moved to Arizona, where he met many other famous Western figures including Pat Garrett, Bat Masterson, and even Billy the Kid. When he was twenty-two, Nat entered a rodeo contest on the Fourth of July in Deadwood, Dakota Territory, and won almost every event, including the rope, throw, tie, bridle, saddle, and bronco riding contests!** After his incredible performance, friends and fans gave him the nickname "Deadwood Dick," and he became a famous character in books and stories written about the Wild West.

After he got married in 1889, Nat decided to settle down. He got a job working on the railroad and moved to Los Angeles where he wrote about the exciting adventures of his life. In 2018, tales of his life were even made into a comic book series. On television, he was portrayed in *The Cherokee Kid*, *They Die by Dawn*, and *Love on the Range*.

No one who ever knew him and no one who ever saw him ever forgot Nat Love, the cowpoke known as Deadwood Dick!

*RUSTLERS ARE PEOPLE WHO TRY TO STEAL CATTLE FROM SOMEONE ELSE'S HERD.

**THE PRIZE WAS $200, WHICH WOULD BE NEARLY $4,700 TODAY.

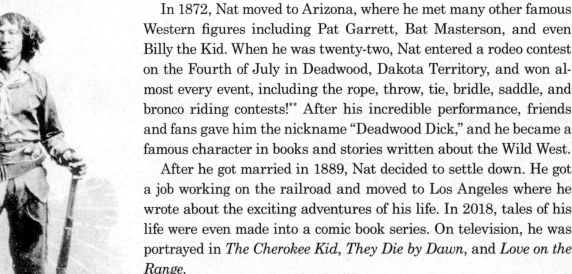

QUICK FACTS	BORN 1854	DIED 1921	CONTRIBUTIONS COWBOY, RODEO STAR, AUTHOR.	STATE: SOUTH DAKOTA

IN 1889, THE DAKOTA TERRITORY, WHERE DEADWOOD WAS LOCATED, WAS DIVIDED INTO TWO STATES: NORTH AND SOUTH DAKOTA. THIS IS THE SOUTH DAKOTA FLAG.

DID YOU KNOW?

Later in his life, Nat (shown here in his uniform) worked as a Pullman porter. Porters helped passengers on and off the train and were also attendants in the sleeping cars.

Black Hills, South Dakota, has two historical monuments carved into mountains: Mount Rushmore, featuring four US presidents, and the Crazy Horse Memorial, in honor of the famous Native American tribal leader.

UNIT: 9TH AND 10TH US CAVALRY

Buffalo Soldiers were black soldiers in the 9th and 10th US Cavalry.* The nickname was given to them by the Native Americans they fought against in the so-called Indian Wars during the late 1800s. During those conflicts, the Buffalo Soldiers fought bravely and won twenty-three Medals of Honor.

In 1877, Henry O. Flipper (see page 48), the first black graduate of West Point, became the first black officer to lead the Buffalo Soldiers. Later, General John J. Pershing, a long-time supporter, led the Buffalo Soldiers in Cuba during the Spanish-American War. In the famous battles of Kettle Hill and San Juan Hill, Buffalo Soldiers were among the first to reach the top.

Buffalo Soldiers also served the country in many other ways, including building roads, protecting the mail, and, thanks to their excellent horsemanship, teaching cadets at West Point how to ride.

Interestingly, Buffalo Soldiers were some of the country's first National Park Service rangers. They built the first road into Sequoia National Park's Giant Forest. They built the first trail to the top of Mount Whitney. And, in Yosemite, they created the first arboretum (tree museum) in America's National Park Service.

One of the first superintendents of Sequoia National Park was Captain Charles Young, the third African American to graduate from West Point. Young supervised enormous projects in the area, and after some time, the residents of the nearby town of Visalia wanted to name a sequoia after Captain Young. Modestly, Captain Young refused, although he later allowed one to be named after his boyhood hero, Booker T. Washington. Recently, however, a sequoia in Giant Forest was, appropriately, named in Captain Young's honor.

Buffalo Soldiers have been featured in many songs, movies, and televisions shows, including *Rawhide*, *The Big Valley*, and *The High Chapparell*. In 1992, future Chairman of the Joint Chiefs of Staff, General Colin Powell, dedicated a statue to honor the Buffalo Soldiers.

*SOLDIERS ON HORSES.

The Booker T. Washington sequoia in Sequoia National Park is one of the largest trees in the world.

QUICK FACTS

CONTRIBUTIONS
FIGHTERS, BUILDERS, TEACHERS, RANGERS.

STATE: LOUISIANA
THE 9TH CAVALRY WAS OFFICIALLY FORMED IN NEW ORLEANS, LOUISIANA. THE STATE WAS NAMED IN HONOR OF KING LOUIS XIV, KING OF FRANCE, AND BECAME PART OF THE U.S. DURING THE LOUISIANA PURCHASE BY PRESIDENT THOMAS JEFFERSON.

IN THEIR
OWN
WORDS:

"WE CAN.
WE WILL."

—9TH CAVALRY
MOTTO

DID YOU KNOW?

The "Smokey the Bear" hat, now synonymous with National Park Service rangers, was introduced by Buffalo Soldiers.

At 14,505 feet tall, California's Mount Whitney is the highest mountain in the U.S. outside Alaska.

5

MEXICAN COWBOYS

CHARROS, VAQUEROS, AND THE CHARREADA

The first cowboys in America were Spanish settlers who had come to Mexico in the 1500s and set up ranches. When the Spanish first settled in Mexico, they were required by the King of Spain to raise cattle and horses—but not allow any of the native people to ride them. However, by 1528, the Spanish had such huge estates (called *haciendas*) that they began to use native people as *vaqueros* (herdsmen). The vaqueros soon became excellent horsemen. By the early 1700s, cattle ranching had spread north into what is now Texas, Arizona, New Mexico, and California, and as far south as Argentina. At one time, perhaps as many as one out of every three cowboys in the Americas was a Mexican vaquero.

Later on, small ranchers became the first people known as *charros*—cowboys with a special style that included the charro suit: a big *sombrero* (hat), a heavily embroidered jacket, and tightly cut trousers.* These charros then created the *charreada*, a Mexican rodeo with riders in exquisite costumes showing off traditional roping and ranch skills.

In a charreada, contestants parade into the arena on horseback in an elaborate opening ceremony, usually accompanied by a *mariachi* band.** There are then nine events for men and one for women. These events involve horsemanship, bull riding, roping, bronco riding, the *escaramuza*—in which women (*charras*) lead their horses in precise, interweaving patterns—and finally, *el paso de la muerte* (the pass of death), when a charro jumps from his horse onto a loose, unbroken horse and tries to ride it until it stops bucking.

In the 1930s, *charrería* became Mexico's national sport. Charrería has been described as "living history," or as an art form drawn from the demands of working life.In 2016, charrería was included in the Representative List of the Intangible Cultural Heritage of Humanity by UNESCO, the United Nations Educational, Scientific, and Cultural Organization.

*THIS LOOK DATES BACK TO THE SPANISH CONQUEST WHEN, TO SHOW HOW RICH THEY WERE, WEALTHY RANCH OWNERS WOULD OUTFIT THEIR COWBOYS WITH FANCY CLOTHING AND SADDLES.

**MARIACHI IS A STYLE OF MEXICAN MUSIC.

COWBOY WORDS

FROM THE SPANISH LANGUAGE

TEN-GALLON HAT
The word *gallon* actually comes from the Spanish word *galón*, which was a narrow braid. A ten-gallon hat was big enough to hold ten braids, not ten gallons of water.

MUSTANG
From the Spanish word *mesteño*, meaning "a wild, untamed horse."

LASSO
From the Spanish word *lazo*, meaning "knotted rope."

RODEO
From the Spanish word *rodear*, meaning "a pen for cattle at a fair or market."

SOMBRERO
The Spanish word for a wide-brimmed hat that gives great protection from the sun.

RANCH
From the Spanish word *rancho*.

BUCKAROO
An English nickname for cowboys but from the Spanish word *vaquero*, which is what cowboys were called. In Spanish, the "v" is often pronounced like a soft "b."

STAMPEDE
From the Spanish word *estampida*.

LARIAT
Another word for lasso, this is from the Spanish word *la reata*, meaning "the rope."

CHAPS
From the Spanish word *chaparreras*, which means the leather coverings over a cowboy's legs.

BRONCO
The same word as the Spanish word *bronco*, meaning a "wild horse."

CORRAL
The same word as the Spanish word *corral*, meaning a "pen for horses or cattle."

THE ESCALANTE EXPEDITION ✦

LEADERS: ATANASIO DOMÍNGUEZ & SILVESTRE VÉLEZ DE ESCALANTE

In 1776, two Spanish priests, Atanasio Domínguez and Silvestre Vélez de Escalante, set out to find a route from Santa Fe, New Mexico, to their mission in Monterey, California. Along the way, they traveled through many unexplored parts of the American West, including present-day western Colorado, Utah, and northern Arizona.

Their mapmaker, Bernardo Pacheco, created maps and descriptions of "lush, mountainous land filled with game and timber, strange ruins of stone cities and villages, and rivers showing signs of precious metals." His maps helped later travelers create the Old Spanish Trail, a route from Santa Fe to Spain's churches and towns along the Pacific coast.

During their journey, Atanasio and Silvestre were helped by Native American guides from the Timpanogos, a Ute tribe, who showed them where to go. The priests gave gifts to the tribe. In return, they were given fresh horses, berries, and dried fish to eat on their journey.

The Timpanogos tribal leader, Chief Turunianchi, was greatly surprised to learn that the Spaniards had traveled safely through Comanche territory. He strongly advised the expedition to turn back and avoid the warlike Comanche. (In fact, the name *Comanche* comes from the Ute word meaning "anyone who wants to fight me all the time.") The Ute even offered the priests land to build houses on for other Spaniards who might come back.

Nevertheless, the priests continued their trip. The expedition wanted to go south to the Colorado River, but they learned from the Native Americans that it was surrounded by a great, deep canyon (the Grand Canyon, in fact) that the group couldn't cross.

Instead, they continued on to California, but when the expedition found that the mountains to California were deeply covered with snow, they had to turn back. Though they never did make it all the way to Monterey, these two courageous priests opened up an incredible new world that had previously been unknown to Europeans.

A map of the area explored by the expedition. The red line shows their route. This map was drawn by hand with ink and watercolor!

Spanish missionaries built a chain of twenty-one missions, or religious outposts, along the California coast. This one is in present-day Carmel, California, near Monterey.

QUICK FACTS

YEAR	CONTRIBUTIONS	STATE: COLORADO
1776	EXPLORERS, CARTOGRAPHERS.	COLORADO'S NAME COMES FROM SPANISH, MEANING "COLORED RED." RED STONE IS COMMON IN THE AREA, AND EVEN THE STATE'S CAPITOL BUILDING USES A ROSE-COLORED MARBLE IN ITS INTERIOR.

IN ANOTHER'S WORDS:

"[IT WAS] ONE OF THE GREAT EXPLORING EXPEDITIONS OF NORTH AMERICAN HISTORY, MADE WITHOUT NOISE OF ARMS AND WITHOUT GIVING OFFENSE TO THE NATIVES THROUGH WHOSE COUNTRY THEY HAD TRAVELED."

—PROFESSOR HUBERT E. BOLTON, HISTORIAN

DID YOU KNOW?

A person who makes maps is called a cartographer.

In Colorado, the expedition found the incredible ruins of Anasazi cliff dwellings. By building underneath a cliff, the Anasazi likely found protection from their enemies.

PATRICIA AND MARTÍN DE LEÓN

To the Tejanos (Mexican Americans living in southern Texas), family was extremely important. And no Tejano family was more important than the De Leóns—one of the founding families of early Texas that changed history in both Texas and Mexico.

Descended from wealthy Spanish aristocrats, Martín De León and Patricia de la Garza De León came north from Mexico in 1799 to start the Rancho Chiltipiquin, a cattle ranch in what is now San Patricio County, Texas. In 1807, their cattle brand—a connected *E* and *J*—became the very first registered cattle brand in what eventually became Texas.

De León's Colony eventually became Victoria, Texas, shown here in an early map.

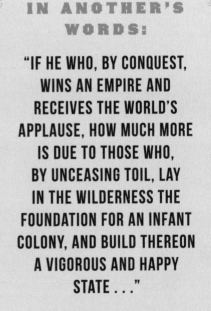

IN ANOTHER'S WORDS:

"IF HE WHO, BY CONQUEST, WINS AN EMPIRE AND RECEIVES THE WORLD'S APPLAUSE, HOW MUCH MORE IS DUE TO THOSE WHO, BY UNCEASING TOIL, LAY IN THE WILDERNESS THE FOUNDATION FOR AN INFANT COLONY, AND BUILD THEREON A VIGOROUS AND HAPPY STATE . . ."

—STEPHEN F. AUSTIN ABOUT MARTÍN DE LEÓN

Later, with money from Patricia's wealthy family, the couple started a community called De León's Colony with forty-one Mexican families. It was the only largely Mexican colony in the eastern part of Texas, which had been mostly settled by immigrants from the United States. Patricia also used her money to build schools and a church and worked to bring a sense of Mexican and Spanish history and culture to the colony.

Like many Tejanos, the De Leóns were opposed to the Mexican dictator Antonio López de Santa Anna and joined the Texas groups that fought against him. One son, Fernando, helped supply guns to Stephen F. Austin (the leader later known as the "Father of Texas"). A daughter, Agustina, married Plácido Benavides, who led Tejano fighters at the Battle of Goliad. He was later recruited by Austin for the Battle of Bexar (now known as San Antonio), where he earned the nickname the "Texas Paul Revere" for riding through the countryside warning people of the approaching Mexican army.

The homes and graves of Martín and Patricia are now Texas landmarks with historic markers that acknowledge the contributions they and their family made to the state's history.

*THE E AND J ARE FROM ESPÍRITU DE JESÚS, SPANISH FOR "SPIRIT OF JESUS."

QUICK FACTS

CONTRIBUTIONS
TEJANOS, FREEDOM FIGHTERS, COMMUNITY BUILDERS.

STATE: COAHUILA Y TEJAS
COAHUILA Y TEJAS WAS ONE OF SEVERAL MEXICAN STATES UNDER MEXICO'S 1824 CONSTITUTION. IT SPLIT, AND THE TEJAS REGION EVENTUALLY BECAME THE US STATE OF TEXAS. THE COAHUILA Y TEJAS FLAG FLEW OVER THE ALAMO ALONG WITH OTHER FLAGS.

Though only Martín is pictured here (it is unknown what his wife looked like), Patricia was an equally powerful force in the family's remarkable accomplishments.

DID YOU KNOW?

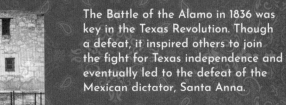

Tejanos is Spanish for "Texan." It was originally used to denote Spanish speaking residents who came from northern Mexican states.

The Battle of the Alamo in 1836 was key in the Texas Revolution. Though a defeat, it inspired others to join the fight for Texas independence and eventually led to the defeat of the Mexican dictator, Santa Anna.

BASS REEVES

NICK NAME: THE INVINCIBLE MARSHAL

Bass Reeves was one of the greatest lawmen of the Wild West. He tracked down, captured, and arrested over 3,000 criminals—more than Wyatt Earp and Wild Bill Hickok put together.

Born into slavery in Arkansas in 1838, Bass escaped during the Civil War into what was then called "Indian Territory." There he lived with the Cherokee, Seminole, and Creek tribes and learned to speak all three Native American languages.

Unfortunately, the land was filled with thieves and murderers. In 1875, Judge Isaac Parker became the federal judge in this huge, lawless area of 75,000 square miles. He picked Bass to help clean it up and made him the first black deputy US marshal west of the Mississippi River. Judge Parker's orders were simple: "Bring 'em in alive—or dead."

IN HIS OWN WORDS:

"MAYBE THE LAW AIN'T PERFECT, BUT WITHOUT IT WE GOT NUTHIN."

Judge Isaac Parker picked Bass Reeves to be the first black deputy US marshal. You didn't want to get on his wrong side—he was famously known as "the hanging judge!"

Six feet, two inches tall, Reeves rode a white stallion and wore two Colt .45 Peacemaker pistols (see page 58) on his hips. Though involved in numerous shootouts, Bass was never wounded, despite once having his hat shot off! Importantly, he never shot a man unless it was necessary to save his own life. Newspapers of the time described him as "absolutely fearless and knowing no master but duty." Above all, Bass had enormous respect for the law. In fact, his code of honor was so great that Bass once even arrested his own son.

More than just an excellent marksman who could shoot with either hand, Bass was an imaginative detective and a master of disguise. He would dress up as a cowboy, farmer, hobo, or even an outlaw to trick criminals into surrendering without firing a shot. And he always left a silver dollar behind as his calling card.

With good manners and a good sense of humor, Bass Reeves was a real celebrity during his life. People loved him and even sang songs about him. Today, many people think he was the model for the Lone Ranger in the 1950s television series. He can also be spotted as a character in books, films, and games.

In 2011, a bridge over the Arkansas River was named for Bass. A statue was erected in his honor at Fort Smith, and in 2013, he was inducted into the Texas Trail of Fame.

QUICK FACTS	BORN 1838	DIED 1910	CONTRIBUTIONS	"INDIAN TERRITORY"
			FIRST BLACK US DEPUTY MARSHALL WEST OF THE MISSISSIPPI.	BEFORE THEY WERE TAKEN OVER AS STATES, HUGE PARTS OF THE AMERICAN WEST CALLED "INDIAN TERRITORY" BELONGED TO NATIVE AMERICAN TRIBES.

DID YOU KNOW?

Many people think the Lone Ranger, a popular radio and television character in the mid-1900s, was based on Bass Reeves. Like Bass, the Lone Ranger rode a white horse. He also used silver bullets as his calling card, not unlike Bass's silver dollars.

The Morgan silver dollar—which Bass Reeves left behind as his calling card—was first minted from 1878-1904 with ninety percent silver and ten percent copper. The model for Miss Liberty was a Philadelphia teacher named Anna Willess Williams.

BIRTH NAME: ELBA MAE GHENT

Mamie jumped hundreds of times with her horses, Babe and Napoleon.

Mamie Hafley performed in Wild West shows and rodeos in acts that required more courage than almost anything anybody else did. In one sharpshooting routine, another woman would shoot at targets on Mamie's hat or sticking out of her mouth! In another, a cowboy and Mamie would ride alongside each other while Mamie shot targets the cowpoke threw in the air.

Most of all, Mamie was famous for her daring, high-diving horse act in which she jumped off a five-story tower into a pool of water on the back of her horse. In her career, Mamie did this hundreds of times all over the nation at state fairs, carnivals, and amusement parks like Dreamland Park on Coney Island, New York, and Young's Million Dollar Pier in Atlantic City, New Jersey.

Incredibly, Mamie and her horse were injured only three times. Once, her horse landed sideways, was knocked out, and almost drowned, though Mamie was not injured. Another time, her horse fell on Mamie and broke Mamie's arm. A last time, Mamie almost died when she was knocked unconscious and pinned by her horse underwater. Even though she nearly drowned, Mamie got back on her horse and went on with the show!

At times, Mamie's real life was as scary as her shows. Once, Mamie was resting in her berth on a train when she heard the porter shouting, "No! No! Oh, please, no!" while an attacker growled, "I'm going to cut your heart out!" Mamie grabbed her pistol from under the pillow, yanked back the curtain, and pointed it at the attacker's head. Cocking the firing pin with a loud click, Mamie said:

"You're not going to cut anybody's heart out!"

Seeing a very steady pistol aimed right between his eyes, the man folded his knife and put it back in his pocket.

In 1981, Mamie Francis Hafley was honored at the National Cowgirl Museum and Hall of Fame in Fort Worth, Texas, the only museum in the world dedicated to celebrating women, past and present, "whose lives exemplify the courage, resilience, and independence that helped shape the American West."

IN HER OWN WORDS:

"IN THE WEST WHERE I WAS RAISED, WOMEN ARE BY NO MEANS THE WEAKER VESSEL."

Do NOT try this at home! Or anywhere!

QUICK FACTS	BORN 1885	DIED 1950	CONTRIBUTIONS PERFORMER, TRAINER.	STATE: WISCONSIN

STATE: WISCONSIN
MAMIE HAFLEY GREW UP MOSTLY IN WISCONSIN. IT WAS THERE THAT SHE SAW AND JOINED HER FIRST SHOW—AND THE REST IS HISTORY.

WISCONSIN
1848

DID YOU KNOW?

Mamie's fifty-foot plunge from a five-story tower ended in a pool only ten feet deep!

In the early 1900s, there were amusement parks all over the United States. Coney Island alone would sometimes have over a million visitors in one day!

HORSE NAMES: GLASS EYE & TAR BABY

A first-class gentleman as well as an incredible horseman, Jesse Stahl started his rodeo career when he was thirty years old. He then kept at it for almost twenty years and gave performances that have become the stuff of legend.

Perhaps Jesse is best remembered for the Salinas Rodeo in California in 1912. In front of 4,000 fans, Jesse stole the show on a wild horse named Glass Eye.* Exploding out of the gate with incredible force, Glass Eye jumped, stomped, bucked, and twisted his entire body in midair circles. No sooner had one end touched the ground than Glass Eye threw the other end up, doing everything he could to throw Jesse to the ground. Indeed, it took all of Jesse's talent and skill to stay in the saddle, but in the end, Glass Eye stopped from exhaustion—and Jesse was the winner.

IN ANOTHER'S WORDS:

"HE SAYS HE CAN RIDE ANYTHING THAT WEARS HAIR."

—*SAN FRANCISCO CHRONICLE*, 1919

Interestingly, years later, the site of the Salinas Rodeo became another scene of racial bias: an assembly camp for the internment of Japanese Americans during World War II.

Despite being one of the highlights of the show, Jesse was, unfairly, given second place. Many people thought it was because he was black. In order to poke fun at the judges' unfair decision, Jesse rode a second bronco—while facing backward! Then he did it again, this time on a notorious bucker called Tar Baby—with a suitcase in his free hand.

As if riding backwards wasn't enough, at other rodeo shows, Jesse and another black cowboy, Ty Stokes, both rode on a single bucking horse seated back to back in what they called a "suicide ride." Stahl also invented "hoolihanding:" leaping from a horse onto a 2,000-pound bull, grabbing its horns, and wrestling it to the ground.**

As one of the greatest bronco riders of all time, in 1979, Jesse was inducted into the Cowboy Hall of Fame—only the second black cowboy (after Bill Pickett) to receive the honor.

*IN THE WEST, NOT JUST THE PEOPLE, BUT EVEN THE HORSES HAD GREAT NAMES.

**HOOOLIHANDING WAS EVENTUALLY OUTLAWED—IT WAS TOO DANGEROUS, NOT FOR THE RIDERS, BUT FOR THE CATTLE!

QUICK FACTS	BORN 1879	DIED 1935	CONTRIBUTIONS RODEO STAR.	STATE: TENNESSEE

TENNESSEE, WHERE JESSE WAS PROBABLY BORN, WAS THE FIRST FEDERAL TERRITORY TO APPLY FOR STATEHOOD TO CONGRESS. ON JUNE 1, 1796, TENNESSEE BECAME THE 16TH STATE OF THE UNION.

DID YOU KNOW?

In the early 1900s, suitcases—like the one Jesse held during his famous ride—were much bulkier and heavier than the ones we use today.

In a rodeo, a rider must stay on a bucking bronco for at least eight seconds with one hand in the air before he or she gets any score.

ALIAS: WILLIAM CATHAY

Government records about Cathay's request for a pension.

Born in Independence, Missouri, to a slave mother and a free father, Cathay was forced to work for the Union Army as a cook and washerwoman during the Civil War. When the war ended, work was hard to get, but Cathay did not want to depend on the charity of friends and relations. She wanted to make her own way in the world—and that's when she got the idea to become a soldier herself.

Since women weren't allowed to join the Army at the time, Cathay Williams flipped her name around to William Cathay and signed up—as a man! Because the average height of men in 1865 was only five foot six and Cathay was five foot nine, and since the Army didn't require full medical exams at the time, Cathay had little problem enlisting. For three years, she served with the new Buffalo Soldiers regiment protecting miners and traveling immigrants. In all that time, only two other soldiers knew the truth about Cathay. One was her cousin and the other was a friend, and both kept her astonishing secret. Thus, she became the first African-American woman to ever enlist in the United States Army.

In 1868, Cathay got smallpox and had to go to the hospital. There, a doctor finally discovered that William Cathay was really Cathay Williams—a woman, not a man—and she had to leave the Army. To top it off, despite her several years of service, Cathay was also denied the soldier's pension that any other man would have received.

Fortunately, history has been more kind to Cathay, and in recent years, many things have been done to recognize her service. In 2016, a bronze sculpture was unveiled in Leavenworth, Kansas. Later, in 2018, the newest addition was unveiled on the Walk of Honor at the National Infantry Museum: a monument bench of Private Cathay Williams.

IN HER OWN WORDS:

> "THE POST SURGEON FOUND OUT I WAS A WOMAN AND I GOT MY DISCHARGE."

As commemorated by the Gateway Arch, Missouri—Cathay's home state—played a big role in the westward expansion of the United States. The Pony Express, Oregon Trail, Santa Fe Trail, and California Trail all began in Missouri.

QUICK FACTS	BORN 1844	DIED 1893	CONTRIBUTIONS SOLDIER, COOK, SEAMSTRESS	STATE: MISSOURI

STATE: MISSOURI
MISSOURI, WHERE CATHAY WAS BORN, WAS ADMITTED IN 1821 AS A SLAVE STATE. DURING THE CIVIL WAR, MISSOURI WAS CLAIMED BY BOTH THE UNION AND THE CONFEDERACY.

DID YOU KNOW?

This pot was used by the 17th Missouri Volunteer Infantry Regiment during the Civil War. It's likely that Cathay Williams used something similar when she worked as a cook for the Union Army.

It was the *St. Louis Daily Times* newspaper that heard of Cathay, tracked her down, and first reported her remarkable story.

GIVEN NAME: LOEB STRAUSS

Born in Germany, Levi* Strauss moved to New York City in 1847. When gold was discovered at Sutter's Mill the next year, the California Gold Rush was on—and more than 300,000 adventurers from all over the world came seeking their fortunes. One was Levi Strauss. But Levi didn't go to pan for gold. His idea was to sell the miners the things they would need—clothing, underwear, umbrellas, handkerchiefs, and canvas tents.

Later, when Jacob Davis, a tailor in Nevada who bought cloth from Levi, came up with an idea to make canvas pants super strong with copper rivets that could stand up to the hard work of mining, the two men started a company making and selling the first jeans.**

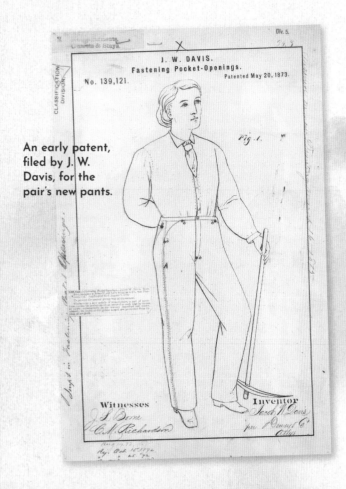

J. W. DAVIS.
Fastening Pocket-Openings.
No. 139,121. Patented May 20, 1873.

An early patent, filed by J. W. Davis, for the pair's new pants.

Witnesses

Inventor

In addition to being a successful businessperson, Levi was very generous with the money his company made. Along with other well-known San Franciscans, he helped build a new railroad, provided the money for twenty-eight scholarships at the University of California, and supported organizations including the Pacific Hebrew Orphan Asylum, the Home for Aged Israelites, the Roman Catholic and Protestant Orphan Asylums, the Eureka Benevolent Society, and the Emanu-El Sisterhood. In fact, Levi was so beloved that when he died, businesses all over San Francisco were temporarily closed so people could go his funeral. The *San Francisco Call* newspaper wrote that Levi's "acts of charity in which neither race nor creed were recognized, exemplified his broad and generous love for and sympathy with humanity." In the end, Levi was a man who was remembered as much for the money he gave away as for the money his businesses made.

*LEVI WAS A STRAUSS FAMILY NICKNAME. HIS REAL NAME WAS LOEB.

**THEY WERE A BIG HIT THEN, AND THERE'S A GOOD CHANCE YOU OWN A PAIR TODAY. THE FIRST JEANS WERE CALLED XX JEANS, BUT LATER THE NAME CHANGED TO 501.

| QUICK FACTS | BORN 1829 | DIED 1902 | CONTRIBUTIONS BUSINESSMAN. CO-CREATOR OF 501 BLUE JEANS. | STATE CALIFORNIA, THE 31ST STATE, ENTERED THE UNION AS A FREE, NON-SLAVERY STATE IN 1850. |

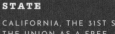
CALIFORNIA REPUBLIC

IN HIS OWN
WORDS:

"AN EXPERT KNOWS
ALL THE ANSWERS—IF
YOU ASK THE RIGHT
QUESTIONS."

DID YOU KNOW?

There were many ways people rushed to California in search of gold. With towering masts and 26,000 square feet of canvas sails, clipper ships were the fastest commercial sailing vessels ever built and could sail from New York to San Francisco in as little as forty-three days. In 1849 alone, over 91,400 passengers sailed to San Francisco from all over the world.

13

JEWS IN THE
AMERICAN WEST

In the 1800s, the American West became home to thousands of people of the Jewish faith who found greater freedom there than they did back East. In this new frontier of opportunity, they became soldiers, freedom fighters, mayors, gunfighters, photographers, businessmen, and even a tribal chief. Here are just a few of their remarkable accomplishments.

SOLOMON BIBO

INDIAN CHIEF

Many Jewish merchants had strong ties with Native American tribes and learned their languages. Married to a woman from the Acoma tribe, Solomon Bibo was elected a tribal chief in 1885. He introduced modern agriculture and started a school for Acoma children.

SOLOMON CARVALHO

EXPLORER, ARTIST, PHOTOGRAPHER

In 1853, Colonel John C. Frémont hired Solomon to take daguerrotypes (early photographs) to show that a central route would be the best path for a transcontinental railroad. Despite the freezing weather and suffering from frostbite, he took pictures that showed the territories of Kansas, Colorado, and Utah, as well as photos of Native Americans the expedition met along the way.

BRONCHO BILLY ANDERSON

MOVIE STAR

In 1903, the star of the first American Western film, *The Great Train Robbery*, was actually a Jewish man from New York named Max Aronson. His role as a rough, tough bandit become so famous that he was put on a US stamp, has a star on the Hollywood Walk of Fame, and is honored in the National Cowboy and Western Heritage Museum.

ADOLPHUS STERNE

REVOLUTIONARY

Adolphus helped the fight for Texas independence by supplying guns to Sam Houston's army through Mexican lines.

SOL STAR

MAYOR

Mr. Star served ten terms as mayor of Deadwood, South Dakota, and helped build the town's first hotel, The Bullock, that is still open today!

JEWISH RANCHERS

Many Jews found opportunity as ranchers in the West. One even used the Star of David as the brand for his cattle.

SIMON SUHLER, DAVID GOODMAN, AND JACOB TRAUTMAN

CAVALRYMEN

Fighting in the Indian Wars, these three frontier cavalrymen were all awarded the Congressional Medal of Honor for bravery.

JOSEPHINE MARCUS

THE GIRL IN THE O.K. CORRAL, WYATT EARP'S WIFE

The gunfight at the O.K. Corral in 1881 was the most famous shootout in Western history. One of the few eyewitnesses was a teenager, Josephine Sarah Marcus, who later married Wyatt Earp. Despite not being Jewish, Wyatt Earp is buried in a Jewish cemetery in Colma, California, where Josephine's family had a plot.

JIM LEVY

GUNSLINGER

Born in Ireland in 1842, Jim Levy ended up in Nevada where he worked as a miner. He soon gave up mining to become a professional gambler and gunslinger all over the West. He was involved in and survived an estimated sixteen shootouts!

BIRTH NAME: WAAYA-TONAH-TOESITS-KAHN

One of the greatest rodeo cowboys ever, Jackson Sundown was a Native American from the Nez-Perce, a tribe famous for horse riding. Not only could he ride horses, Jackson could even ride buffalo. Once, after he rode a bull that no one else had been able to, the bull refused to ever buck again. In fact, Jackson was so good at bronc bustin' and bull riding that many other riders would simply withdraw from a rodeo when they found out he was in it.

Although Jackson learned to breed and raise horses at an early age, his most famous moments came during the 1911 roundup* in Pendleton, Oregon, when he was fifty-three. Although twice the age of most other competitors, Jackson entered the roundup and agreed to ride a notoriously fierce horse named Angel.

ABOUT JACKSON SUNDOOWN:

"CROWDS HAVE NEVER SEEN SUCH SPLENDID HORSEMANSHIP."

—IDAHO NEWSPAPER

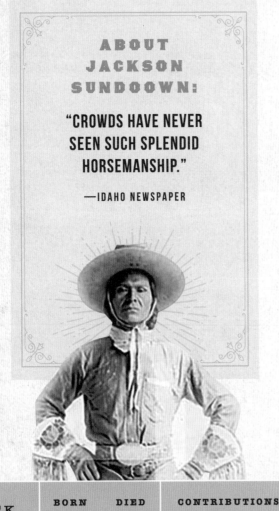

Even though Angel bucked furiously, twisted in circles, and exploded into the air, Sundown stayed on the whole time—until the judges signaled the end of the ride. At that point, Sundown got off the horse, took off his hat, and fanned Angel to cool him down. Even though the wild horse was exhausted, Jackson looked as neat and cool as he had when he got on. The judges announced, "Jackson Sundown, first place!" and the crowd went wild.

A huge crowd favorite, Jackson not only rode better than other cowboys, but with his brightly colored shirts, fancy chaps, and long braids tied under his chin, Jackson looked better, too.

Featured in a novel about the Pendleton Round-Up, *The Last Go 'Round*, Jackson was inducted into the American Indian Athletic Hall of Fame, the National Multicultural Western Heritage Museum and Hall of Fame, and the National Cowboy and Western Museum and Hall of Fame. Even today, people who love the rodeo still talk and write about Jackson's legendary feats that took place over one hundred years ago.

*ROUNDUP IS ANOTHER WORLD FOR RODEO.

| QUICK FACTS | BORN 1863 | DIED 1923 | CONTRIBUTIONS GREATEST RODEO STAR OF ALL TIME. | STATE: OREGON OREGON, HOME OF THE PENDLETON ROUNDUP, BECAME THE 33RD STATE IN 1859 WITH A CONSTITUTION THAT PROHIBITED SLAVERY BUT STILL PREVENTED FREE BLACKS FROM LIVING THERE. | |

DID YOU KNOW?

Jackson was so famous, there are sculptures of him in the Radio City Music Hall in New York and on Pendleton, Oregon's "Bronze Trail."

"Nez Perce" was the name given this large group of indigenous people by French fur traders. It means "pierced nose," even though few of them actually had pierced noses.

NICK NAME: STAGECOACH MARY

"Stagecoach" Mary Fields was one of the most amazing characters of the Old West and a beloved role model, then and now, for women, African Americans, and everybody else! Six feet tall and 200 pounds, Mary worked as a cook, carpenter, wood chopper, farmer, and the forewoman of St. Peter's Mission in the Montana Territory.

But most of all, Mary was famous for delivering the mail. Mary got her nickname when she was sixty-three years old. She won a competition for a mail job by being the fastest person to hitch a team of six horses to a stagecoach. This made her the second woman and first African American woman to work for the US Postal Service.

For six years, Mary Fields rode a stagecoach packed with letters, money, and expensive parcels through the wild Montana territories. Mary would deliver anything, anywhere, anytime, through any kind of weather and every kind of danger. Braving blizzards, heat waves, driving rain, and howling winds, Mary never missed a day of work, never failed to deliver a single letter, and was never late once! Even if the snow was too deep for her horses, it didn't stop Mary. She would tie the horses to a tree and walk on snowshoes, carrying the sacks on her shoulders.

Once, she was attacked by a pack of wolves that scared her horses and overturned her carriage. Through the night, Mary fought the wolves with her shotgun and revolver. In the morning, she pushed the carriage upright, rounded up a few of her horses, and delivered food and medicine to a convent of nuns.

Mary became such an admired person that the town she lived in, Cascade, Montana, closed its schools to celebrate her birthday each year. Years later, Mary was portrayed in television shows and movies, but she will be remembered best as the stalwart pioneer who was as tough as she was kind.

IN HER OWN WORDS:

"I LOVE ADVENTURE. I TRAVEL THE COUNTRY. NOBODY TELLS ME WHAT TO DO. NOBODY TELLS ME WHERE TO GO. I LIKE TO BE ROUGH. I LIKE TO BE ROWDY. I ALSO LIKE TO BE LOVING. I LIKE TO BE CARING. I LIKE TO BABY SIT. I LIKE TO PLANT FLOWERS AND TEND MY GARDEN. I LIKE TO GIVE AWAY CORSAGES AND BOUQUETS. I LIKE BEING ME, MARY FIELDS."

The name Montana comes from the Spanish word *montaña*, meaning "mountain" or "mountainous country."

QUICK FACTS	BORN 1832	DIED 1914	CONTRIBUTIONS MAIL CARRIER, FREIGHT HAULER, FOREWOMAN.	STATE: MONTANA MONTANA, WHERE MARY LIVED AND WORKED, BECAME THE 41ST STATE IN 1889. IT IS HOME TO THE COUNTRY'S FIRST NATIONAL PARK: YELLOWSTONE.

MONTANA

DID YOU KNOW?

Mary loved baseball. She regularly gave small bouquets from her garden to the local team's players.

Mary moved to Montana in order to take care of a family friend, Mother Mary Amadeus (pictured here), who had pneumonia. Mother Amadeus later helped Mary start her own restaurant, but it closed within in a year because Mary gave so much food away for free to those in need.

JAMES BUTLER HICKOK

NICK NAME: WILD BILL HICKOK

Photographs of Wild Bill seem to show him with dark hair, but it was really red.

No book about the West would be complete without "Wild Bill" Hickok. Born in Illinois, Bill's father was an abolitionist who helped slaves escape through the Underground Railroad. During the Civil War, Bill spied for the Union Army and was later a scout for both General George Custer and the Buffalo Soldiers.

Known as an outstanding shot, Wild Bill was elected marshal in Hays, Kansas. After becoming involved in several famous shootouts, all of which he won, Bill brought order to the wild city.

Once, while trying to control a rowdy crowd during a street brawl, Bill ordered the leader of the gang arrested for firing a pistol in the city limits. Ignoring Bill's order, the man turned his gun on Hickok. Wild Bill drew instantly, fired first, and the man fell to the ground. Turning to the crowd of drunken cowboys who were with the man he'd just shot, Hickok said:

"Now do any of you fellows want the rest of these bullets?"

No one said a single word.

Later, Wild Bill became marshal of Abilene, Kansas, another "cowtown" at the end of the famous Chisolm Trail. There, he met other famous figures of the West, including Buffalo Bill, the gunslinger John Hardin,*** and Calamity Jane, who fell in love with him. Once again, Bill was an effective lawman and brought order to a dangerous town.

Unlike his life in law enforcement, Hickok's life as a showman was not so successful. When he put on a show in Niagara Falls called "The Daring Buffalo Chasers of the Plains" with six Native Americans, six buffalo, a bear, and a monkey, the buffalo escaped from their pen and chased screaming members of the audience all around the grounds.

Not surprisingly, the show flopped.

Later, when Buffalo Bill invited Wild Bill to join his show, he often hid behind the scenery and once even shot out the spotlight when it was pointed at him. Clearly, he didn't enjoy acting and soon left the show.

Sadly, in 1876, Wild Bill was shot from behind while playing poker. He was holding two pairs: black aces and black eights. Poker players now call this the "Dead Man's Hand."

Almost the entire town attended Bill's funeral.

Wild Bill is still one of the most popular figures of the Old West and has been featured in movies, books, radio shows, and a television series called *The Adventures of Wild Bill Hickok*.

*BILL WAS ORIGINALLY CALLED "DUCK BILL" BECAUSE HIS LIPS REMINDED PEOPLE OF A DUCK. UNDERSTANDABLY, HE CHANGED IT TO WILD BILL. WOULDN'T YOU?

**IT WAS A VERY TOUGH JOB. BEFORE BILL CAME TO TOWN, THREE SHERIFFS HAD QUIT IN JUST EIGHTEEN MONTHS.

***ONCE, HARDIN SHOT A MAN IN A HOTEL "FOR SNORING TOO LOUD."

The Kansas motto, "Ad Astra per Aspera," is Latin for "To the Stars Through Difficulties."

QUICK FACTS	BORN 1837	DIED 1876	CONTRIBUTIONS LAWMAN, SCOUT, RELUCTANT ACTOR.	STATE: KANSAS

STATE: KANSAS
KANSAS, WHERE WILD BILL WAS A SHERIFF, WAS ADMITTED TO THE UNION IN 1861. AT ONE TIME, THE STATE HAD A LAW AGAINST SERVING ICE CREAM ON CHERRY PIE.

KANSAS

IN HIS OWN WORDS:

"I CAME TO THE CONCLUSION THAT . . . THE BOLDEST PLAN IS THE BEST AND THE SAFEST."

DID YOU KNOW?

Buffalo, like the ones who chased Wild Bill's terrified audience, were once plentiful in the United States. At the beginning of the 1800s, there were tens of millions of buffalo across North America.

Wild Bill was the subject of many stories and cartoons. Here, he's shown after his famous shoot-out with gambler Davis Tutt.

REAL NAME: MARTHA JANE CANARY

There's no question that nicknames in the Wild West were flat-out cool, from Wild Bill Hickok and Billy the Kid to Deadwood Dick and Bronco Sam. Maybe the greatest nickname, though, was given to Martha Jane Canary: Calamity Jane. There are many different explanations of how she got it. Some say it was from a wounded soldier after she saved his life during an Indian attack. Other people think it was because she was fiercely independent and told anyone who crossed her that they were "courting calamity."* Whatever the explanation, Jane really was wild and free; she told everybody exactly what was on her mind and did whatever she wanted. She dressed like a man and could shoot like one, too. Indeed, when she came into the town of Deadwood with Wild Bill Hickok's wagon train, she was so famous that it was *her* arrival which was announced in the local newspaper with the headline: "Calamity Jane Has Arrived!"

No question, Jane had guts. Once, when the driver of a stagecoach was shot with an arrow, Jane took the reins from his dying hands and drove the coach to safety, saving the lives of the other six passengers (all men, by the way). Another time, she swam the Platte River and rode her horse ninety miles at top speed, while cold and wet, to deliver important messages for the Army.

Jane was just as generous as she was bold. Though she was only fourteen when her parents died, Jane raised her brothers and sisters all by herself. Later, as a grown woman, she nursed the victims of a deadly smallpox epidemic back to health, even at the risk of losing her own life.

After a life of excitement and adventure, Calamity Jane was featured in Buffalo Bill's** Wild West show as a rider, sharpshooter, and storyteller who told the unforgettable tales of her incredible life. And, thanks to her big personality and warm-hearted spirit, the legend of Calamity Jane has lived on in books, television shows, cartoons, songs, and over ten movies.

*THE WORD *CALAMITY* MEANS DISASTER. "COURTING CALAMITY" MEANS LOOKING FOR TROUBLE.

**BUFFALO BILL CODY: ANOTHER GOOD NICKNAME, UNLESS YOU WERE A BUFFALO.

IN HER OWN WORDS:

"I FIGURE IF A GIRL WANTS TO BE A LEGEND, SHE SHOULD GO AHEAD AND BE ONE."

"CALAMITY JANE" IN 1885 (*Above*)
I FOUND "CALAMITY" SMOKING A CIGAR AND COOKING BREAKFAST (*Below*)

QUICK FACTS

BORN	DIED
1852	1903

CONTRIBUTIONS
FRONTIERSWOMAN, EXPLORER, ARMY SCOUT, PERFORMER.

STATE
NEBRASKA, WHERE CALAMITY JANE SWAM THE PLATTE RIVER, IS HOME TO CHIMNEY ROCK, THE LANDMARK MOST OFTEN MENTIONED IN THE JOURNALS OF OREGON TRAIL PIONEERS.

DID YOU KNOW?

After her death, Calamity Jane was buried next to the famous Wild Bill Hickok (see page 40). Some say the two were married, but the evidence is unclear.

Traveling in a stagecoach was very uncomfortable, but it was often the safest way to travel in the West before the railroads.

WAGON TRAINS

Imagine traveling over rough country in a wagon with wooden wheels and metal rims. Imagine feeling every bump go up your spine and through your body with every pothole you hit. Imagine your face being burned by the sun and lashed by the wind, rain, and snow. Imagine crossing frigid streams, scorching deserts, and steep ravines. Imagine all this for several months and over a thousand miles, and you'll have some idea how tough the people who went West in wagon trains were. They were survivors who would do whatever it took to make their lives better and follow their dreams.

Wagon trains began heading west in the early 1820s and hit their peak in the 1850s during the California Gold Rush. Typically starting in Independence, Missouri, they followed routes like the Santa Fe Trail, the Chisholm Trail, the California Trail, the Mormon Trail, and the Old Spanish Trail. The longest was the Oregon Trail, which was over 2,000 miles long. Between 1830 and 1870, the Oregon Trail and its offshoots were traveled by about 400,000 settlers, farmers, miners, ranchers, and business owners and their families.

Wagon trains usually included farm wagons fitted with metal hoops and covered with canvas for protection. Despite the name, wagon trains didn't usually travel in a line like a train, since that would create a lot of dust for the wagons at the back. Whenever possible, they went side by side. Also, while wagon trains did often form a circle at night to keep animals from running away or being stolen, wagon-train masters rarely called out "circle the wagons" to protect a train from attack. That's mostly the stuff of Hollywood cowboy movies.

Given the hardships and slowness of wagon-train travel, after the transcontinental railroad was completed in 1869, travel by wagon train was understandably reduced to almost nothing, although a lot of modern highways and railroads now run parallel to large parts of the famous old trails.

In 1852, there were records of a wagon train from Illinois to California with 1,500 turkeys in tow.

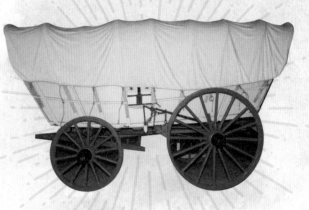

Despite being in many cowboy movies, Conestoga wagons, like the one pictured here, were actually too heavy to be good in wagon trains.

Wagon trains usually had around thirty wagons traveling together, though some had as many as 200.

Amazingly, some wagon ruts along the well-traveled trails are still visible today. The ones pictured to the right are in Oregon Trail Ruts State Historic Site near Guernsey, Wyoming.

Many railroads now run alongside parts of the old wagon trails.

NICK NAME: THE SINGING COWBOY

GOODBYE, OLD PAINT

GOODBYE OLD PAINT
I'M LEAVING CHEYENNE
GOODBYE OLD PAINT
I'M LEAVING CHEYENNE

OLD PAINT'S A GOOD PONY
SHE PAYS US WHEN SHE CAN
GOODBYE OLD PAINT
I'M LEAVING CHEYENNE

MY HORSES AIN'T HUNGRY
THEY WON'T EAT YOUR HAY
MY WAGON IS LOADED
AND ROLLING AWAY

WHEN I TAKE MY SADDLE
DOWN FROM THE WALL
PUT IT ON MY PONY
LEAD HIM FROM THE STALL
TIE MY BONES TO HIS BACK
TURN OUR FACES WEST
WE'LL RIDE THE PRAIRIE
THAT WE LOVE THE BEST

GOODBYE OLD PAINT
I'M LEAVING CHEYENNE
GOODBYE OLD PAINT
I'M LEAVING CHEYENNE

"He had a knack for singing. He had a gift, if you will. His voice was real soothing to the cattle, and this is why they wanted him to participate in these big cattle drives, because he would sing to them and just make them relax."

—Franklin Willis, Charley's great-grandson, in a National Public Radio interview

Born into slavery near Austin, Texas, Charley Willis became a free man after the Civil War. A skilled horseman by the age of eighteen, Willis went to west Texas, where he found work "breaking" wild horses (making them tame enough to ride). Later, Charley became a cowhand who rode the Chisholm Trail as a drover* taking herds of Texas cattle north.

More than anything, Charley was a talented singer. He wrote the popular song "Goodbye Old Paint."** Over his life, Charley became known for this and many other songs he wrote as well as tunes he'd heard cowboys sing out on the trail. To help keep authentic cowboy music alive for all of us, Charley unselfishly passed along all these songs on to other musicians, which is a big part of the reason we still know them today. In 1885, for instance, Willis taught "Goodbye Old Paint" to a seven-year-old Texas boy, Jess Morris, who later grew up to become a talented fiddler and band leader.

In 1947, when he was sixty-nine, Mr. Morris was recorded playing and singing "Goodbye Old Paint," which is now in the American Folklife Center at the Library of Congress. You can hear him play and sing the tune on You Tube at www.youtube.com/watch?v=DRyhbVO8cQI. It's simple and scratchy, but remember: this is exactly the tune cowboys used to sing at night under the big, Western sky.

*A DROVER IS A PERSON WHO DRIVES CATTLE OVERLAND TO A MARKET WHERE THEY CAN BE SOLD.

**HIS HORSE'S NAME WAS, INDEED, OLD PAINT.

QUICK FACTS

BORN	DIED	CONTRIBUTIONS	STATE: TEXAS
1847	1930	COWBOY, SINGER, SONGWRITER.	WITH ITS SINGLE WHITE STAR, THE FLAG OF TEXAS LED TO THE STATE'S NICKNAME: "THE LONE STAR STATE."

DID YOU KNOW?

The Chisholm Trail was established by Native American cattle rancher Black Beaver and Jesse Chisholm, a Scottish-Cherokee fur trader.

Charley rode the Chisholm Trail from Texas to Abilene, Kansas, where cattle were shipped east by railroad.

RANK: SECOND LIEUTENANT

In 1877, Henry Ossian Flipper became the first African American to graduate from the United States Military Academy at West Point. He later became the first non-white officer to lead the Buffalo Soldiers of the 10th Cavalry (see page 16).

The first black officer to command regular troops in the US Army, Henry was given high marks for his leadership during the Apache Wars and Victorio Campaign. Later, Henry's commanding officer, Captain Nolan, made him his chief officer and Henry was given command of this unit by himself.

IN HIS OWN WORDS

"I ASK ONLY THAT JUSTICE WHICH EVERY AMERICAN CITIZEN HAS THE RIGHT TO ASK."

Unfortunately, because he was friendly with Captain Nolan's daughter, there were officers who wanted to get him kicked out of the Army. Henry was set up to make it look like he was stealing. As a result, he was unfairly dismissed from military service. Happily, in 1999, almost a century later and years after his death, Henry was pardoned and given the honorable discharge he'd earned.

Henry wasn't just an accomplished military leader. He was also a skilled engineer.[*] At Fort Sill, Oklahoma, he created a system to drain a swamp which had caused many soldiers to suffer from malaria.[**] Known as "Flipper's Ditch," it quickly helped eliminate the disease. Today, it still controls floods and erosion as part of Fort Sill's Historic Landmark and National Register Historic District.

After the Army, Henry served as assistant to Secretary of the Interior Albert W. Fall. He worked in Mexico and Latin America, writing legal and scientific works and translating Mexican Land Laws and Venezuela's Law on Hydrocarbons. He also published numerous books, including *The Colored Cadet at West Point and Black Frontiersman: The Memoirs of Henry O. Flipper, First Black Graduate of West Point*.

In 1977, a statue of Henry was unveiled at West Point. Since then, an annual Henry O. Flipper Award has been granted to graduating cadets at the academy who exhibit "leadership, self-discipline, and perseverance in the face of unusual difficulties."

[*]LT. FLIPPER IS WIDELY CONSIDERED THE FIRST AFRICAN AMERICAN CIVIL AND MINING ENGINEER AND WAS A MEMBER OF THE ASSOCIATION OF ARIZONA CIVIL ENGINEERS.

[**]SPREAD BY MOSQUITOES, MALARIA IS A DISEASE WITH A HIGH FEVER AND SHAKING CHILLS. EVEN TODAY, MALARIA KILLS HUNDREDS OF THOUSANDS OF PEOPLE AROUND THE WORLD EVERY YEAR.

QUICK FACTS	BORN 1856	DIED 1940	CONTRIBUTIONS OFFICER, ENGINEER, SCIENTIST, AUTHOR, DIPLOMATIC AIDE.	STATE: NEW YORK THE US MILITARY ACADEMY AT WEST POINT IS IN NEW YORK STATE NEXT TO THE HUDSON RIVER. NEW YORK'S FLAG ALSO FEATURES THE HUDSON RIVER.

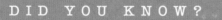

DID YOU KNOW?

The United States Military Academy at West Point was established in 1802. It graduated many military leaders, including Robert E. Lee, Ulysses S. Grant, Dwight D. Eisenhower, and Buzz Aldrin.

Controlling malaria was crucial to many construction projects, like the Panama Canal. Many workers during these projects died not from accidents, but from illness.

WILLIAM FREDERICK CODY

NICK NAME: "BUFFALO BILL" CODY

William Frederick "Buffalo Bill" Cody was probably the most famous person in the Old West. Born in Iowa, he was a rider for the Pony Express by the age of fourteen. He then became a ranch hand, builder, fur trapper, gold prospector, wagon train driver, Army scout, and marksman. He got his nickname from hunting buffalo to feed the workers who were building the Kansas Pacific Railway.

A playing card signed by Buffalo Bill.

IN HIS OWN WORDS

"MY RESTLESS, ROAMING SPIRIT WOULD NOT ALLOW ME TO REMAIN AT HOME VERY LONG."

Above all, Bill was an entertainer who put together one of the greatest shows on earth: Buffalo Bill's Wild West and Congress of Rough Riders of the World. With cowboys, Native Americans, gauchos,* Arabs, and Mongols dressed in their native costumes, the show featured sharpshooters, horse races, rodeo events, and sideshows. Many famous figures, such as Annie Oakley, Calamity Jane, and the Native American chief, Sitting Bull, were part of the spectacle as it toured the United States and the world.

In 1887, the show went to Great Britain, where Queen Victoria loved it and royalty from all over Europe attended. Later, the show went to Paris, where it was part of the Exposition Universelle,** and then on to Rome, where Buffalo Bill met Pope Leo XIII. At the time, Mark Twain called Buffalo Bill the biggest celebrity on earth.

Just as important as his showmanship, Buffalo Bill supported numerous good causes. As a conservationist, he spoke out against "hide-hunting" (shooting buffalo just for their coats) and spoke up for the establishment of a hunting season. He also supported the rights of women, including equal pay for equal work and the civil rights of Native Americans. He paid his Native American performers well and urged them to bring their families on tour. Since many people at the time thought poorly of Native Americans, Bill encouraged his Native American performers to set up teepees and camps so people could see how they and their families were just like everyone else.

Over the years, Buffalo Bill Cody has been portrayed in many, many books, plays, movies, and television shows.

For his service in the Army, he was given the Medal of Honor, and as an exceptional honor, Buffalo Bill was featured on two US postage stamps.

*A GAUCHO IS A COWBOY FROM ARGENTINA.

**THIS WAS ALSO THE DEBUT OF THE EIFFEL TOWER.

QUICK FACTS

BORN	DIED	CONTRIBUTIONS	STATE: IOWA
1846	1917	SOLDIER, SCOUT, SHOWMAN.	IN 1846, IOWA, WHERE BUFFALO BILL WAS BORN, BECAME THE 29TH STATE. IT'S THE BIRTHPLACE OF ANOTHER FAMOUS WESTERN ICON: ACTOR JOHN WAYNE.

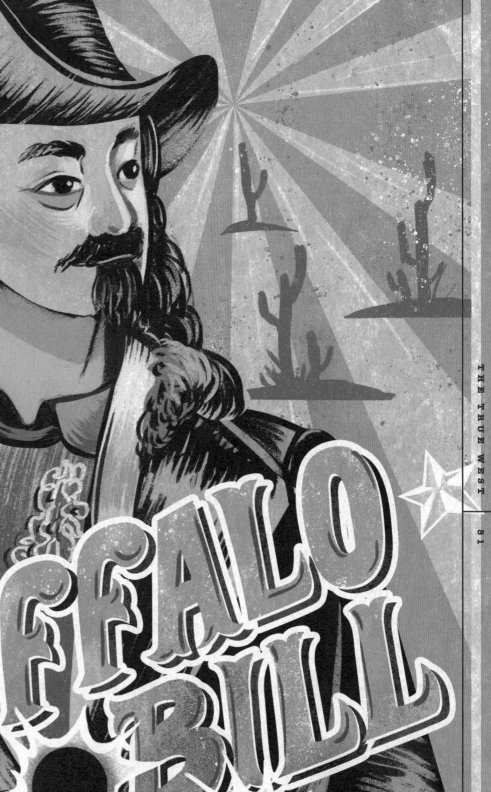

BUFFALO BILL

DID YOU KNOW?

In colonial times, Iowa was part of French Louisiana. Its flag is patterned after the French tricolor flag.

Buffalo Bill's Wild West was a hit all over the world. (And by the way, the word "show" was not part of the program's name.)

PRETTY AS A PICTURE.
TOUGH AS NAILS.

When she was sixteen, Fox Hastings ran away from a convent school in California and began an incredible career as a rodeo superstar. At the time, women couldn't even vote (except in Wyoming), but in the rodeo world, things were different. Rodeo stars were North America's first professional female athletes and they earned far more than women in other fields. By the end of her long career, Fox was both wealthy and famous.

Wherever she went, Fox wowed fans, won praise, and broke records. As a trick rider, she could stand on the fastest ponies at full gallup. She was even one of the first and only women to ever "bulldog" a steer*—jump from a running horse, grab the steer by the horns, and bring it down to the ground! During her first year of bulldogging, Fox set a record when it took her just seventeen seconds to wrestle a steer to the mud. Later, at the Cattlemen's Convention in Houston, she was named the most outstanding act of the entire Texas Rodeo—including both men and women.

Even though she was a true beauty with ribbons in her hair and a bandana around her shoulders, Fox was a genuine daredevil—courageous and determined. Once, even though she had broken a rib, she went out and bulldogged three days in a row! Another time, after her horse fell on top of her, Fox got up, hopped on another horse, and completed her ride to loud applause. After all, she had a contract to fulfill—and Fox always made good on her promises.

In 1987, Fox Hastings was inducted into the National Cowboy Hall of Fame in Oklahoma City. In 2011, she was honored by the National Cowgirl Museum and Hall of Fame in Fort Worth, Texas.

IN HER OWN WORDS

"IF I CAN JUST GET MY FANNY OUT OF THE SADDLE AND MY FEET PLANTED, THERE'S NOT A STEER THAT CAN LAST AGAINST ME."

*BULLDOGGING WAS EVENTUALLY OUTLAWED, NOT BECAUSE OF THE OBVIOUS DANGER TO THE COWGIRL WHO MADE THE LEAP, BUT BECAUSE SOMETIMES THE STEERS WERE KILLED. BULLDOGGING WAS FIRST DONE BY BILL PICKETT (SEE PAGE 10).

The press didn't always know what to say about the women who competed with other cowboys. Said one newspaper about Fox: "To the rodeo crowd she is Fox Hastings, cowgirl extraordinaire. To neighbors she is Mrs. Mike Hastings, a good cook and tidy housekeeper."

QUICK FACTS	BORN 1898	DIED 1948	CONTRIBUTIONS TRICK RIDER, BULLDOGGER, RODEO STAR.	STATE: ARIZONA

STATE: ARIZONA

IT TOOK FIFTY-SIX YEARS FOR ARIZONA, WHERE FOX DIED, TO BECOME THE 48TH STATE, WHICH FINALLY HAPPENED IN 1912. THE THIRTEEN RAYS OF RED AND GOLD REPRESENT BOTH THE THIRTEEN ORIGINAL COLONIES AND THE RAYS OF THE WESTERN SETTING SUN.

DID YOU KNOW?

Arizona's state flower is really a tree—the saguaro cactus—which can grow over forty feet tall!

Fox performed all over the country, from Los Angeles to Madison Square Garden in New York City (now the home of the New York Knicks basketball team).

NICK NAME: BRONCO SAM

Born in Mexico of mixed African, Mexican, and European ancestry, Sam Steward came north from Texas with the very first herd of cattle brought to Wyoming. His trail boss, Bill Walker, said Sam "wasn't afraid of anything and could ride everything." In fact, Sam was just about as wild as the broncs he rode.

But one day, in 1870, his crew decided that horses just weren't enough. They roped the biggest longhorn in the herd, put a saddle on it, and challenged Sam to ride it through the town of Cheyenne. Sam jumped on the steer and rode it down the main street with his crew whooping and hollering and swinging knotted ropes to drive the bucking steer along.

Texas longhorns are half wild and hard to control. They weigh between 1,400 and 2,500 pounds.

IN HIS OWN WORDS

"I BROUGHT OUT A SUIT FOR EVERYBODY IN THE CREW!"

Of course, Sam's steer was frightened and wild-eyed. When it saw itself reflected in the window of a clothing store, it stopped for a second, pawed the ground, then busted right through the window, charging down the aisles, over the counter, and around the shelves. Sales clerks dove for cover while the steer plunged through the store's clothing racks. When the steer charged back outside, Sam was still in the saddle and the steer's horns were decorated with just about everything in the store—pants, coats, hats, and even underwear! When he was still riding the steer covered with clothes, Sam shouted, "I brought out a suit for everybody in the crew!"

After Sam returned the steer to the herd, he hopped on his horse and went back into town. When the understandably unhappy owner of the store came out to meet him, Sam just smiled, apologized, and asked politely what the damages were. The shopkeeper got the books and figured out the bill. When Sam was told the price was $350, he never batted an eye. He just peeled off $350 in cash and handed it over.

Wyoming's name comes from a Munsee word, xwé:wamənk, that means "at the big river flat."

QUICK FACTS	BORN 1852	DIED 1888	CONTRIBUTIONS COWBOY, DAREDEVIL.	STATE: WYOMING

STATE: WYOMING

WYOMING, WHERE SAM BROUGHT THE VERY FIRST HERD OF CATTLE, IS STILL THE LEAST POPULOUS STATE IN THE UNITED STATES. IT WAS THE FIRST STATE TO LET WOMEN VOTE!

DID YOU KNOW?

$350 in 1875 would be about $7,636.59 today!

24

CHINESE RAILROAD WORKERS

While they weren't cowboys, Chinese workers unquestionably helped build the West. In the beginning, many Chinese men came to the U.S. to mine gold. If they didn't strike it rich, they often got work building the new railroads that tied the United States together. In 1865, fifty Chinese immigrants were hired to work on the Central Pacific Railroad—a 1,912-mile rail line that would connect California to Nebraska as the western part of the First Transcontinental Railroad in the United States. These workers did such a good job that the railroad company eventually hired more than 12,000 Chinese workers. Indeed, at one time, eight out of ten people working on the Central Pacific Railroad were Chinese!

The Central Pacific and Union Pacific railroads were joined together in 1869 at Promontory Summit, Utah Territory. A crew of Chinese and Irish men had laid the last ten miles of track in just twelve hours!

Working from dawn to dusk in the worst weather, the Chinese workers laid tracks in dangerous areas for extremely low pay. In the steep mountains, these workers solved problems with innovations they had learned in China, like lowering men in baskets from the tops of cliffs to plant explosives to blast tunnels. Often forced to live in the tunnels they were building or to sleep in shelters they carved out of deep snow, more than one thousand died in accidents and avalanches.

Finally, however, in 1869, the western railway met up with the half that was being built from the eastern side of the country. A golden spike was hammered into place to connect the two railways at Promontory Point, Utah, in front of a cheering crowd and a band. The new railroad made it possible to cross the country in eight days instead of taking long sea voyages or dangerous trips in wagon trains.

Despite their incredible accomplishments, the Chinese workers were often persecuted by most other people—even the US government. It wasn't until 1991, nearly one hundred years later, that a monument near Colfax, California, was built to recognize the important contributions of the Chinese in creating the railway that had changed the country. Without question, they were among the bravest, most hardworking people in the American West. Without firing a shot or riding a horse, these workers were genuine heroes who helped make this country a better place to live.

The final spike connecting the two railroads was made of gold. It was driven in by Leland Stanford. Stanford was the president of Central Pacific Railroad, governor of California, and founder of Stanford University.

CONTRIBUTIONS
BUILDERS OF THE WEST.

STATE: UTAH
UTAH, WHERE THE TRANSCONTINENTAL RAILROAD WAS FINALLY COMPLETED, GETS ITS NAME FROM THE UTES, THE REGION'S NATIVE TRIBE. IN THE TRIBE'S LANGUAGE, UTE MEANS "LAND OF THE SUN."

DID YOU KNOW?

In 1867, forty-four storms brought over forty feet of snow!

The Summit Tunnel took 8,000 men over two years to build, going through 1,750 feet of solid granite at a rate of 1.82 feet a day.

25

CLOTHES

THE STETSON

The first real cowboy hat, the Stetson—also called the "Boss of the Plains"—was creased right down the center of the crown with a dent on each side, making it easy to take off. It was immediately popular and became the iconic image of cowboys in the Old West. Before this, there was no standard cowboy hat; most cowboys wore old Civil War hats, derbies, and even top hats.

COWBOY VESTS

Since riding on a horse made it hard to get into pants pockets, the vest was added with deep pockets to store things.

COWBOY JACKETS

Heavy canvas jackets protected against the weather and from thorn and cactus spines while riding through the desert.

BLUE JEANS

Levi Strauss (see page 32) introduced jeans—durable, canvas pants with rivets—in 1868. The first jeans were actually brown, not blue.

THE COLT "PEACEMAKER"

The most popular gun used by cowboys was the Colt .45, a revolver with an eight-inch barrel that could hold six bullets.

TEN-GALLON HAT

Actually, a ten-gallon hat will only hold about three quarts of water (see page 18)! In the Southwest, these hats had tall crowns to help keep a cowboy cool and wide brims to protect the eyes and the skin against the fierce sun. In the North, brims were narrow and crowns lower so they would not blow away in the wind.

THE BANDANA

Tied around the neck, the bandana could be lifted to cover the mouth and nose from the dust of cattle drives. They were also used as washcloths, to mop the sweat from the brow, and to prevent sunburn.

CHAPS

From the word *chaparejos*, chaps were long leggings worn over pants for protection against thorns and cactus.

GUN BELT

Worn loose and low on the hip, the belt had loops for about fifty cartridges and, with the gun, weighed several pounds.

COWBOY BOOTS

With two-inch Cuban heels to keep the boots in the stirrups or to dig into the ground while roping a calf, cowboy boots were great riding boots but not so good for walking.

FURTHER READING

FOR KIDS

To learn more about some of the people and events in this book, consider these other titles:

ANNIE OAKLEY

Spinner, Stephanie. *Who Was Annie Oakley?* New York, NY: Grosset & Dunlap, 2002.

BILL PICKETT

Pinkney, Andrea Davis., and J. Brian Pinkney. *Bill Pickett, Rodeo-Ridin Cowboy*. San Diego: Harcourt Brace, 1999.

BUFFALO SOLDIERS

Baker, Brynn. *Buffalo Soldiers: Heroes of the American West*. North Mankato, MN: Capstone Press, a Capstone imprint, 2016.

CHINESE RAILROAD WORKERS

Fraser, Mary Ann. *Ten Mile Day and the Building of the Transcontinental Railroad*. New York: Square Fish/Henry Holt and Company, 2012.
Perritano, John. *The Transcontinental Railroad*. New York: Childrens Press, 2010.

CATHAY WILLIAMS

Solomon, Sharon K., Doreen Lorenzetti, and Cathay Williams. *Cathay Williams, Buffalo Soldier*. Gretna: Pelican, 2010.

JACKSON SUNDOWN

Fisher, Doris, and Sarah Cotton. *Jackson Sundown: Native American Bronco Buster*. Gretna: Pelican Publishing Company, 2018.

LEVI STRAUSS

Johnston, Tony, and Stacy Innerst. *Levi Strauss Gets a Bright Idea: A Fairly Fabricated Story of a Pair of Pants*. Boston: Harcourt Childrens Books, 2011.

MARY FIELDS (STAGECOACH MARY)

Charles, Tami, and Claire Almon. *Fearless Mary: Mary Fields, American Stagecoach Driver*. Chicago, IL: Albert Whitman & Company, 2019.

MEXICAN COWBOYS

Freedman, Russell. *In the Days of the Vaqueros: America's First True Cowboys*. New York: Clarion Books, 2001.

Sandler, Martin W. *Vaqueros: Americas First Cowmen*. New York: H. Holt and Co., 2001.

NAT LOVE

McKissack, Pat, Fredrick McKissack, Randy DuBurke, and Nat Love. *Best Shot in the West: The Adventures of Nat Love*. San Francisco: Chronicle Books, 2012.

WAGON TRAINS

Gregory, Josh, and Farré Lluís. *If You Were a Kid on the Oregon Trail*. New York, NY: Childrens Press, an Imprint of Scholastic Inc., 2017.

WILLIAM FREDERICK CODY (BUFFALO BILL CODY)

Warren, Andrea. *The Boy Who Became Buffalo Bill: Growing Up Billy Cody in Bleeding Kansas*. New York: Amazon Publishing, 2015.

PHOTO AND ART CREDITS

Cover: border (Roberto Castillo/Shutterstock.com), turquoise textures (Antracit/Shutterstock.com), boots (Jamie Depledge/Shutterstock.com), background landscape (Library of Congress/2018696539); **Endpapers:** Nature painting (Library of Congress/2004667227), Buffalo Bill (Library of Congress/94507313), Bill Pickett (Library of Congress/92500459), Gordon's (Library of Congress/2005694416), cattle painting (Library of Congress/2018695491), fair illustration (Library of Congress/2018695484), Union Pacific (Public domain), black cowboys (Texas State Historical Association [Public domain]), Calamity Jane (imprint of C.E. Finn, Livingston, Mont. [Public domain]), Buffalo soldiers (Everett Historical/Shutterstock.com), Texas state seal (grebeshkovmaxim/Shutterstock.com), Colorado and Oklahoma state seals (michal812/Shutterstock.com), railroad tunnel (Library of Congress/ca2410); **General:** decorative page border (Harry Kasyanov/Shutterstock.com), paper texture (Lukasz Szwaj/Shutterstock.com), quotation box border (Vasya Kobelev/Shutterstock.com), US state flags (grebeshkovmaxim/Shutterstock.com), campfire (VoodooDot/Shutterstock.com), bandana pattern (Labetskiy Alexandr/Shutterstock.com), watercolor textures (Godsend/Shutterstock.com), vintage radial bursts (monkographic/Shutterstock.com), contents icons (various Shutterstock.com artists: Mechanic Design, Marco's studio, vectorchef. Vector Icon Flat, StockAppeal, veronawinner, 10EPS ICON, Martial Red), Calamity Jane (Library of Congress/2016649829), vaqueros (Library of Congress/2002719127), Chinese workers (Library of Congress/2005682913), Buffalo Soldier (Library of Congress/2010645138); **Bill Pickett:** movie poster (Norman Films [Public domain]), Bill Pickett (Photographer unknown. "Courtesy North Fort Worth Historical Society" [Public domain]), film reel (Graeme Dawes/Shutterstock.com), bull (Roberto Cerruti/Shutterstock.com), bull icon (davooda/Shutterstock.com); **Annie Oakley:** Annie Oakley (Baker's Art Gallery, Columbus, Ohio [Public domain]), Buffalo Bill poster (Public domain), Annie Oakley Harpers Weekly (Peter Newell [Public domain]), Thomas Edison (Public domain), playing card (Alis Photo/Shutterstock.com), playing card icon (Venomous Vector/Shutterstock.com); **Nat Love:** Nat Love (Public domain), Nat Love as porter (Public domain), Mount Rushmore (Jess Kraft/Shutterstock.com), *Deadwood Dick* book cover (Public Domain), book icon (AVIcon/Shutterstock.com); **Buffalo Soldiers:** Buffalo soldier (Public domain), giant sequoia (davidhoffmann photography/Shutterstock.com), Buffalo soldiers group (Chr. Barthelmess [Public domain]), hat (Maksym Bondarchuk/Shutterstock.com), Mount Whitney (Johnny Adolphson/Shutterstock.com), hat icon (Sudowoodo); **The Escalante Expedition:** map (Library of Congress/96686648), mountains (f11photo/Shutterstock.com), map right (Public domain), Anasazi cliff dwellings (Gleb Tarro/Shutterstock.com), mountains icon (Jacky Co/Shutterstock.com), Carmel Mission (Burkhard Mücke [CC BY-SA (https://creativecommons.org/licenses/by-sa/4.0)]); **Patricia and Martín De León:** map (Herman Brosius, [Public domain]), Alamo (Sean Pavone/Shutterstock.com), Texas icon (Alice July/Shutterstock.com), Coahuila y Tejas flag (Froztbyte [CC BY-SA (https://creativecommons.org/licenses/by-sa/3.0)]); **Mexican Cowboys:** Mexican flag (Magi Bagi/Shutterstock.com); **Bass Reeves:** Bass Reeves (Public domain), Judge Parker (Mathew Brady [Public domain]); Lone Ranger (Pleasure Island), Morgan silver dollar (Brandon Grossardt for the coin image. George T. Morgan for the coin design. [Public domain]), sheriff icon (Ctrl-x/Shutterstock.com); Mamie Hafley: Mamie Hafley (SMU Central University Libraries), diving (Library of Congress/2012645715), water pool (Peangdao/Shutterstock.com), Coney Island ferris wheel (Brooklyn Museum), diving pool icon (AVIcon/Shutterstock.com); **Jesse Stahl:** Jesse Stahl (Oregon Historical Society/OHS12526), suitcase (Skoda/Shutterstock.com), bucking bronco (Margo Harrison/Shutterstock.com), suitcase icon (IhorZigor/Shutterstock.com), Salinas Assembly Center (National Archives at College Park [Public domain]); **Cathay Williams:** Army pension records (National Archives), Gateway Arch (Semmick Photo/Shutterstock.com), cooking pot (Missouri History Museum [Public domain]), St. Louis Times building (Boehl and Koenig [Public domain]), Civil War icon (Meth Mehr/Shutterstock.com); **Levi Strauss:** Levi Strauss (Public domain), patent (National Archives), clipper ship (James E. Buttersworth [Public domain]), Levi Strauss & Co (Cullen328 photo by Jim Heaphy [CC BY-SA (https://creativecommons.org/licenses/by-sa/3.0)]), jeans icon (matsabe/Shutterstock.com); **Jews in the American West:** Native American headdress (anttoniart/Shutterstock.com), Solomon Carvalho (Solomon Nunes Carvalho [Public domain]), Broncho Billy Anderson (Motography [Public domain]), Adolphus Sterne (Mayflower Pilgrim 332/FindAGrave.com), Sol Star (Internet Archive Book Images [No restrictions]), Star of David (sreewing/Shutterstock.com), Star of David texture (Maurus Spescha/Shutterstock.com), Congressional Medal of Honor (Gary Todd from Xinzheng, China [CC0]), Josephine Marcus (Public domain), playing cards (Stephen Rees/Shutterstock.com); **Jackson Sundown:** rodeo (Pendleton USA), Jackson Sundown (Oregon Historical Society [Public domain]), Radio City Music Hall (UpstateNYer [CC BY-SA (https://creativecommons.org/licenses/by-sa/3.0)]), Nez Perce (George Catlin [Public domain]), trophy icon (pambudi/Shutterstock.com); **Mary Fields:** Mary Fields (Public domain), flowers (TheGraphicsFairy.com), Mother Mary Amadeus (Public domain), envelope icon (Pavel Stasevich/Shutterstock.com); **James Butler Hickok:** James Butler Hickok (George G. Rockwood [Public domain]), buffalo (Eric Isselee/Shutterstock.com), cartoon (Harper's Weekly, Public domain), Kansas landscape (Wayne Greer/Shutterstock.com); gun icon (Ctrl-x/Shutterstock.com); **Calamity Jane:** Martha Jane Canary top (imprint of C.E. Finn, Livingston, Mont. [Public domain]), Martha Jane Canary at home (*Down the Yellowstone*, Louis R. Freeman [Public domain]), Martha Jane Canary bottom (C.E. Finn, Livingston, Montana [Public domain]), stagecoach (umnola/Shutterstock.com), envelope (KMNPhoto/Shutterstock.com), stagecoach icon (Rvector/Shutterstock.com); **Wagon Trains:** wagon icon (AVIcon/Shutterstock.com), turkeys (photomaster/Shutterstock.com), Mormon Trail (Everett Historical/Shutterstock.com), Conestoga wagon (B&O Museum Collections [CC BY (https://creativecommons.org/licenses/by/2.0)]), wagon train (Everett Collection/Shutterstock.com), Oregon Trail Ruts State Historic Site (Paul Hermans [CC BY-SA (https://creativecommons.org/licenses/by-sa/3.0)]), train icon (umanuma/Shutterstock.com); **Charley Willis:** guitar (schankz/Shutterstock.com), map (Adrian W. Ziegelasch, 1893–1930, download and cleanup by Steve Meirowsky [Public domain]), music icon (davooda/Shutterstock.com); **Henry O. Flipper:** Henry Flipper top (US GOVT [Public domain]), Henry Flipper bottom (U.S. House of Representatives. Committee on Military Affairs. (03/13/1822 - 1946) [Public domain]), West Point symbol (United States Military Academy [Public domain]), Panama Canal workers (Otis Historical Archives Nat'l Museum of Health &Medicine [CC BY (https://creativecommons.org/licenses/by/2.0)]), sword icon (a Sk/Shutterstock.com); **William Frederick Cody:** Buffalo Bill top (George Eastman House Collection [Public domain]), Buffalo Bill bottom (Buffalo Bill Center of the West [Public domain]), French flag (Mr Doomits/Shutterstock.com), poster (Courier Litho. Co., Buffalo, N.Y. [Public domain]), tent icon (yut548/Shutterstock.com), playing card (Fedekuki [CC BY-SA (https://creativecommons.org/licenses/by-sa/3.0)]); **Fox Hastings:** Fox Hastings top (Amon Carter Museum of American Art), Fox Hastings bottom (Montana Memory Project), saguaro cactus (Ufuk ZIVANA/Shutterstock.com), Madison Square Gardens (Public domain), cow icon (DStarky/Shutterstock.com); **Sam Steward:** Longhorn cattle (Quinn Calder/Shutterstock.com), mountains (aceshot1/Shutterstock.com), money (Office of the Comptroller of the Currency and the Bureau of Engraving and Printing [Public domain]), shirt icon (bluebloom/Shutterstock.com); **Chinese Railroad Workers:** Promontory Summit (Andrew J. Russell [Public domain]), golden spike (Wjenning [CC BY-SA (https://creativecommons.org/licenses/by-sa/3.0)]), snow (LilKar/Shutterstock.com), Summit Tunnel (Michael Kahn/www.mklibrary.com), railroad track icon (the Proicon/Shutterstock.com); **Clothes:** Stetson (C.Aphirak/Shutterstock.com), vests (Georgia Evans/Shutterstock.com), jackets (Ysbrand Cosijn/Shutterstock.com), blue jeans (crystalfoto/Shutterstock.com), Colt "Peacemaker" (CreativeHQ/Shutterstock.com), cowboy (Library of Congress/2008678055), boot icon (Jamie Depledge/Shutterstock.com).

SOURCES

For a list of sources consulted and additional reading, please visit www.bushelandpeckbooks.com.

ABOUT THE AUTHOR

Bestselling author, singer, songwriter, and musician Mifflin Lowe has had ten books published, selling over 300,000 copies in five languages. His books include many children's books—*Beasts by the Bunches* (Doubleday); *Z-Z-Z-Z-Z-Z-Z-Z-Z: A Bedtime Story*; *Little Dog, Big Bark*; *Wilton Wilberry and the Magical Christmas Wishing Well*; and *Cowboy Howie: The Adventure of the Central Park Coyote and Thanksgiving Day Parade* (Locokids)—and three humor books for adults: *The Cheapskate's Handbook*, *I Hate Fun*, and *How To Be A Celebrity* (Price/Stern/Sloan.) He has also performed his music for family audiences from New England to New Orleans, presenting works from his children's CDs *The King Who Forgot His Underpants*, *Wilton Wilberry and the Magical Christmas Wishing Well*, and *Beasts by the Bunches* (Caedmon/Harper& Row). Recently, his animated film script, *The Awesome, Amazing, Occasionally Astonishing Adventures of Cowboy Howie*, won the blue ribbon prize in the Sarasota Film Office TV/ME competition.

ABOUT THE ILLUSTRATOR

Wiliam is an illustrator and graphic designer. He graduated from Dong Nai College of Decorative Arts as one of the top students in his class. His work is included in many books including *50 Real Heroes for Boys* (Bushel & Peck).

THE MUSIC OF DOM FLEMONS

If you love the heroes in this book, you'll love the music of Dom Flemons. Grammy-Award winner, two-time Emmy nominee, and 2019 Wammie-Award winner, Dom Flemons is originally from Phoenix, Arizona, and currently lives in the Washington, DC, area. He is known as "The American Songster" since his repertoire of music covers over one hundred years of American folklore, ballads, and tunes. Flemons is a music scholar, historian, record collector, and a multi-instrumentalist. His album, *Dom Flemons Presents Black Cowboys*, sheds light on the music, culture, and complex history of the golden era of the Wild West. In this single volume of music, the first of its kind, Dom Flemons explores and reanalyzes this important part of our American identity. You can hear Dom sing about Bass Reeves (see page 24) here: https://youtu.be/-HxVabgy2hM. You can also check out his newest release at https://omnivorerecordings.com/shop/prospect-hill/ and follow his career at www.TheAmericanSongster.com.

ABOUT BUSHEL & PECK BOOKS

Bushel & Peck Books is a children's publishing house with a special mission. Through our Book-for-Book Promise™, we donate one book to kids in need for every book we sell. Our beautiful books are given to kids through schools, libraries, local neighborhoods, shelters, nonprofits, and also to many selfless organizations who are working hard to make a difference. So thank you for purchasing this book! Because of you, another book will find itself in the hands of a child who needs it most.

WHY LITERACY MATTERS

We can't solve every problem in the world, but we believe children's books can help. Illiteracy is linked to many of the world's greatest challenges, including crime, school dropout rates, and drug use. Yet impressively, just the presence of books in a home can be a leg up for struggling kids. According to one study, "Children growing up in homes with many books get three years more schooling than children from bookless homes, independent of their parents' education, occupation, and class. This is as great an advantage as having university educated rather than unschooled parents, and twice the advantage of having a professional rather than an unskilled father."[1]

Unfortunately, many children in need find themselves without adequate access to age-appropriate books. One study found that low-income neighborhoods have, in some US cities, only one book for every three hundred kids (compared to thirteen books for every one child in middle-income neighborhoods).[2]

With our Book-for-Book Promise™, Bushel & Peck Books is putting quality children's books into the hands of as many kids as possible. We hope these books bring an increased interest in reading and learning, and with that, a greater chance for future success.

NOMINATE A SCHOOL OR ORGANIZATION TO RECEIVE FREE BOOKS

Do you know a school, library, or organization that could use some free books for their kids? We'd love to help! Please fill out the nomination form at our website and we'll do everything we can to make something happen.

www.bushelandpeckbooks.com/pages/nominate-a-school-or-organization

1   M.D.R. Evans, Jonathan Kelley, Joanna Sikora & Donald J. Treiman. Family scholarly culture and educational success: Books and schooling in 27 nations. *Research in Social Stratification and Mobility*. Volume 28, Issue 2, 2010. 171-197.

2   Neuman, S.B. & D. Celano (2006). The knowledge gap: Effects of leveling the playing field for low- and middle-income children. *Reading Research Quarterly*, 176-201.

1.   Pacing Stallion.
2.   Orloff Stallion.
3.   Thoroughbred Stallion.
4.   Pereberon Stallion.
5.   Shire Stallion.

6.   French Coach-Stallion.
7.   Shetland Pony.
8.   Hackney Stallion.
9.   Cleveland Bay stallion.
10.   Belgian Stallion.

11.   Trotting Stallion.
12.   Arab Stallion.
13.   German Coach-Stallion.
14.   Clydesdale Stallion.
15.   Suffolk Stallion.